Ellis Island

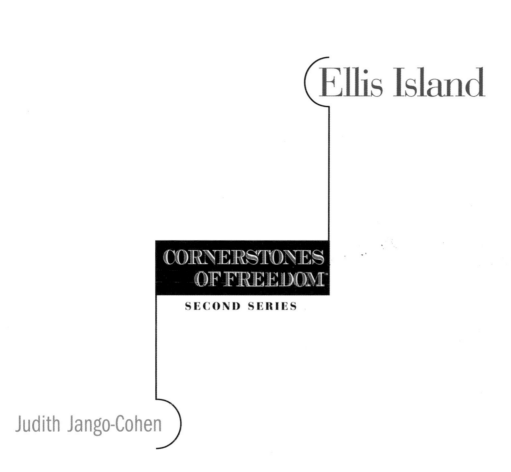

CORNERSTONES
OF FREEDOM

SECOND SERIES

Judith Jango-Cohen

Children's Press®
An Imprint of Scholastic Inc.
New York • Toronto • London • Auckland • Sydney
Mexico City • New Delhi • Hong Kong
Danbury, Connecticut

Photographs © 2005: AP/Wide World Photos: 40 bottom (Stephen
Chernin), 7, 26, 27, 32, 33, 36; Corbis Images: cover top, 3, 10, 14, 19,
24, 28, 34, 35, 37, 38, 39, 45 bottom left (Bettmann), 8 (Hulton-Deutsch
Collection), cover bottom, 40 top (Bill Ross), 6, 11; Eliot Cohen: 22, 45
bottom right; Library of Congress: 15 (via SODA), 4, 5, 9, 16, 17, 18, 21,
29, 31, 44 bottom, 44 top right, 44 top left, 45 top; National Archives and
Records Administration: 23; National Park Service, Statue of Liberty
National Monument: 12, 13, 20, 25, 30, 45 center; Superstock, Inc.: 41.

Library of Congress Cataloging-in-Publication Data
Jango-Cohen, Judith.
  Ellis Island / Judith Jango-Cohen.
      p. cm. — (Cornerstones of freedom. Second series)
  Includes bibliographical references and index.
    ISBN-13: 978-0-516-23625-4 (lib. bdg.)   978-0-531-20833-5 (pbk.)
    ISBN-10: 0-516-23625-3 (lib. bdg.)   0-531-20833-8 (pbk.)
        1. Ellis Island Immigration Station (N.Y. and N.J.)—History—
Juvenile literature. 2. United States—Emigration and immigration—
History—20th century—Juvenile literature. 3. Immigrants—United
States—History—20th century—Juvenile literature. I. Title. II. Series.
  JV6484.J36 2005
  304.8'73—dc22
                                            2004011131

7 8 9 10 R 17 16 15 14 13 12

It is 1907. A small girl stands at the railing of a ship, gripping a ball of yarn in her hands. On shore, another girl holds the end of the yarn. As the ship slips away, the ball of yarn unwinds. The girls do not hear the passengers' good-bye cries. They do not see the waving handkerchiefs or the babies lifted high. Each watches her friend shrinking smaller and smaller. Soon the last bit of yarn flies from the traveler's hands. It flutters above the ship, waving on the wind. The girl's tears dry in the salty air as her home in Italy disappears.

Nine days later the ship enters New York Harbor in the United States of America. America is where many passengers hope to make a new home. Most will pass through Ellis Island. On the island, they will receive permission to stay in America or they will be turned away.

The **immigrants** carry battered baskets and bulging sacks, holding precious pieces of their past. A young woman has packed a photograph and a strand of hair from her baby who has died. Others bring symbols of their faith, such as a golden cross or a silver menorah. People have packed favorite books, tin soldiers, dolls, and musical instruments. They take hand-stitched clothes and down quilts.

From 1892 to 1954, Ellis Island served as the gateway to the United States for millions of immigrants.

A Polish immigrant carries a single trunk with his most prized possessions.

There are also those with no belongings. One Jewish family, fleeing from Russia, has borrowed an empty suitcase. They do not want others to know that they have nothing. But even those with no possessions carry three things with them. Each person brings courage, hope, and a story.

In 1915, a group of Armenian children board a ship. They are leaving to seek safety in other countries.

THE GREAT ESCAPE

A Russian girl hides in her basement, struggling to quiet her baby sister. Soldiers have come to rob the house and kill her family because they are Jewish. Cleverly, her father has set out bottles of whiskey to distract the soldiers. While the soldiers drink, the family slips away. During the night, they hurry to the train station. The train takes them to a seaport where they board a ship to America.

In the late 1800s and early 1900s, millions of immigrants left their homelands in Europe and journeyed to America. Some, such as Russian Jews, fled from religious or racial **persecution**. The Armenians in Turkey were another such group. In March 1915, the Muslim Turkish government announced a decision to rid Turkey of all the Christian Armenians. Some Armenians were murdered in their homes. Others were marched into the desert, where they died of hunger or thirst. Between 1915 and 1923 the Turkish government killed more than one million Armenians.

These two Dutch children arrived on Ellis Island in 1906.

Hunger drove other immigrants across the sea to America. Europe's population was growing, and there were not enough jobs for everyone. People in cities found it difficult to feed their families. In the countryside, wealthy people owned much of the farmland. People who worked for them earned barely enough money to survive.

Some immigrants came because harsh rulers gave them little freedom in their own countries. Benito Mussolini, for example, controlled the government in Italy. He also controlled the newspapers, radio programs, and movies, allowing no one to speak out against him.

★　★　★　★

Benito Mussolini came to power in Italy in 1922. Some Italians left their country to escape his harsh rule.

* * * *

The United States became a refuge for people from many countries. In America, immigrants bought land and started their own farms. In growing cities, they found jobs building roads, bridges, and parks. They voted for the leaders of their choice. They were free to say what they believed, and they worshipped as they pleased. Escaping death and despair, they found freedom from want and freedom from fear.

Millions of immigrants left their homes, friends, and sometimes families in hopes of building a better life in the United States.

GOD BLESS AMERICA

Many immigrants felt that coming to America was like opening a door to a new life. For immigrants who could not speak English and had no education, that life was difficult.

But hardships did not break them. In fact, many immigrants became famous. Songwriter Irving Berlin was a Russian Jew who came to the United States in 1893. He would later write one of our country's most beloved songs, "God Bless America."

9

THE IMMIGRATION STATION

Immigrants sailed into seaports throughout America. They arrived in cities such as Boston, Baltimore, Philadelphia, New Orleans, Seattle, and San Francisco. The nation's biggest and busiest port was New York.

Swamped with immigrants, New York was the first of these ports to open a receiving station. In 1855, the state set up Castle Garden on the southern tip of Manhattan. At Castle Garden, immigrants could exchange their own money for American dollars. They could also buy railroad tickets to other cities. If they were staying in the city, they could obtain information about jobs and housing there.

A group of immigrants arrives in New York Harbor in 1878.

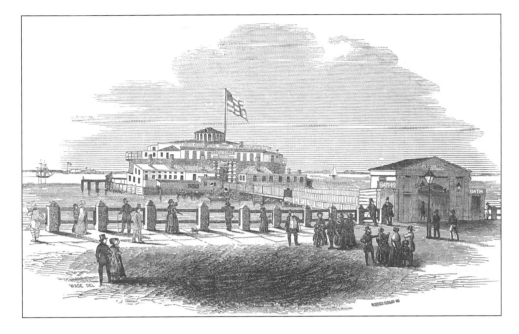

Between 1880 and 1900 about nine million immigrants entered the United States. These record-breaking waves of immigrants made some Americans uneasy. They wanted laws passed to control the number of people who could enter the country.

In 1891, the United States government created the Bureau of Immigration. This organization would take charge of the immigration process. The government also passed a law rejecting certain immigrants, including criminals, people with a serious **contagious** disease, and those who could not support themselves due to mental or physical illness.

New York was receiving about 75 percent of America's immigrants. As a result, it needed a bigger immigration station. Some people felt that the harbor islands would be an ideal location. There, people could be kept off the mainland

★ ★ ★ ★

This photograph shows Ellis Island in 1897, before the fire.

while being inspected for admission to America. Bedloe's Island, now called Liberty Island, was suggested, but it was already home to the Statue of Liberty. Instead, the honor fell to its neighbor Ellis Island, about 1 mile (1.6 kilometers) west of Castle Garden.

Construction of the Ellis Island Immigration Station began in 1890. In January 1892, the immigration station was completed. Twelve new buildings stood on the island, including the main receiving building, four hospital buildings, a restaurant, and a kitchen.

The station did not serve immigrants for long. One June evening in 1897, people looking across the water at Ellis

Island saw a startling sight. The *New York Sun* reported, "Flames were shooting a hundred feet in the air, and by their light hundreds of people could be seen on the island running hither and thither." Luckily, the inspection station was not busy. Ferries rescued the staff and all 140 immigrants. But the wooden station was a charred ruin.

One month after the fire, construction began on a new immigration station. The Barge Office, near Castle Garden, served as a receiving station during this time. The new brick and stone building, still standing today, opened on December 17, 1900.

The Barge Office was used as a temporary immigration station from 1897 to 1900.

THE EARLY YEARS

Ellis Island was a busy place even before it became home to the immigration station. Samuel Ellis, a businessman, owned the land during the American Revolution. In 1810, the United States government bought the island and built a fort. The fort guarded New York Harbor during the War of 1812. After the war Ellis Island was used as a place to store **explosives**. Nearby residents of New Jersey and New York were relieved to see the explosives removed for the construction of the immigration station.

13

* * * *

THE JOURNEY

When the new immigration station opened in 1900, airplanes did not yet exist. Immigrants had to travel across the sea in ships. Before the 1920s most ships sold three types of tickets: first-class, second-class, and steerage.

First-class tickets were the most expensive. Wealthy passengers stayed in roomy cabins with running water. They ate in dining rooms and were served fancy meals that were cooked by skilled chefs. Second-class passengers stayed in similar cabins that were slightly less grand.

The least expensive way to travel on most ships was in **steerage**. The steerage area was in the dark "basement" of the boat near the steering equipment. Before the 1920s

In 1920, more than two thousand Italian immigrants crowd the deck of the S.S. *Regina de Italia* for their first glimpse of the U.S.

there were no cabins in steerage. It was simply an open area lined with rows of bunks. By 1922, ships had built third-class cabins in their lowest levels.

Most immigrants could afford only steerage. Some shipping companies stuffed in two or three times as many people as could reasonably fit. Passengers slept on mattresses made from bags of straw or seaweed. Life preservers became pillows. Often, toilets were just a pit. Steerage was usually never cleaned, even though people ate and slept there. The smell was so thick and strong, people felt as if they could touch it.

Conditions aboard the steamships were not ideal. Tired men, women, and children endured dirty, overcrowded conditions for weeks at a time.

Some shipping companies let passengers set sail on leaky boats. Many people, especially children, got sick on these waterlogged ships. Because of the wet, filthy conditions, they sometimes died. With horror, immigrants watched as the crew threw the small bodies of children into the water.

Other more fortunate people had happy memories of their voyage. Children swung on rope swings that sailors set up

15

Children play onboard the *Friedrich der Grosse*, a German ship.

for them. Some played with pets that they had sneaked onboard. Others gathered together to sing and recite poems. Even people speaking different languages managed to feel close. One man said that when people patted him on the head or gave him a hug, he knew they were friends.

Most immigrants met stormy weather on their voyage. Choppy waves made many people seasick. But bad weather could do something much worse—it could sink a ship. As heaving seas tossed the boat up and down, passengers prayed and cast religious medals into the water. One woman and her brother remember being told that their ship was likely to go down. But the misery they had been through in their own country had taught them to have courage. So when the sailor gave them the terrifying news, the two responded, "We will dance."

Somehow, their storm-battered ship stayed afloat. When it later sailed into New York Harbor, people streamed toward the railing to see the Statue of Liberty. "Please, everybody, we should move a little bit to the center!" the captain pleaded. He feared that the unbalanced ship would surely sink. But everyone was crying, and nobody moved. Jews stood in their prayer shawls, and Christians knelt,

The Statue of Liberty was many immigrants' first welcome to the U.S.

STOWAWAYS

Most ships had stowaways hiding onboard. The most determined stowaway held at Ellis Island was fourteen-year-old Michael Gilhooley. Gilhooley was a Belgian boy whose mother had died during World War I. In 1919, Gilhooley stowed away five times, hoping to start a new life in America. Each time he was discovered and returned to Belgium. American newspapers printed his story, and hundreds offered to help. Finally, officials placed him in the care of a wealthy New York woman. Soon the former stowaway was riding through the city in a fancy limousine.

Ship officials search for stowaways among the baggage.

making the sign of the cross. One woman remembers seeing the Statue of Liberty opening her arms to all the immigrants. The woman begged the beautiful lady to give her a chance to do something, to be somebody in America.

ENTERING ELLIS ISLAND

People sailing into New York may have felt that the Statue of Liberty was welcoming them to America, but they hadn't been accepted just yet. First, the inspectors of the Bureau

18

★　★　★　★

of Immigration had to decide if an immigrant was "clearly and without a doubt **entitled** to land."

When a ship anchored in the harbor, doctors and inspectors went out to meet it. Doctors separated all who were sick and sent them to hospitals on the island. Those with contagious diseases were sent into New York City until a contagious disease hospital opened at the station in 1911.

Immigrants with scarlet fever are removed from the S.S. *Lapland* and brought to the hospital at Ellis Island.

★ ★ ★ ★

Inspectors briefly questioned the first- and second-class passengers. Most were quickly cleared because the government saw little risk in admitting these wealthy people to the United States. When the boat docked, they were free to go. Steerage and third-class passengers had to endure a more lengthy inspection on Ellis Island.

Sometimes thousands of immigrants arrived at once. People had to wait aboard ship for hours or even days until a barge could take them to the island. Friends and family already living in America sometimes passed by in little boats. Immigrants lowered baskets to the boats and hauled up treats from their visitors.

Steerage passengers had to undergo lengthy questioning by Ellis Island officials.

Immigrants board a ferry that will take them to Ellis Island.

When the ship was allowed to dock, people boarded a barge to Ellis Island. If the inspection station were full, people waited on these barges. "We were jammed in so tight that I couldn't turn 'round," one immigrant recalled. Besides being crowded, barges lacked enough seats, drinking water, and toilets. They also provided no protection from summer sun or winter winds.

At last, people stepped onto Ellis Island. All had different impressions as they entered the castle-like building with copper-domed towers. One man described it as big enough to hold everyone in his village as well as their cattle. Many remembered the confusion of boxes, bundles, and endless rows of benches. There were babies screaming, children running, and nervous families huddled

THE GOLDEN DOOR

The Statue of Liberty has graced New York Harbor since 1886. A poem called "The New Colossus" is inscribed on the pedestal. It was written by Emma Lazarus, an author who was inspired by the courageous immigrants seeking freedom in America. Its most famous lines read:

Give me your tired,
* your poor,*
Your huddled masses
* yearning to*
* breathe free,*
The wretched refuse of
* your teeming shore.*
Send these, the homeless,
* tempest-tost to me,*
I lift my lamp beside the
* golden door!*

The Statue of Liberty was a gift from France to the United States. It serves as a symbol of the liberty both countries treasure.

together. Inspectors with blue coats and brass buttons dashed back and forth.

The uniformed watchmen and doctors scared many immigrants. Their uniforms reminded some people of the police and soldiers who had persecuted them back home. One man explained that in his country, a person in uniform was not someone who would help him. It was someone who might cut off his head.

MEDICAL EXAMS

Upon entering the immigration station, everyone lined up for a medical exam. Doctors watched immigrants for signs of limping, unsteadiness, and difficulty breathing. They inspected skin and scalp for infections. Doctors also

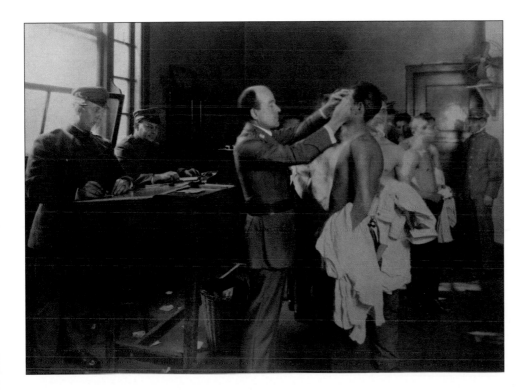

Doctors perform physical checkups on male immigrants at Ellis Island.

questioned people to check their hearing and speech. If immigrants did not speak English, **interpreters** helped out.

Other doctors examined people's eyes. They were on the alert for diseases like trachoma. This contagious infection could cause blindness if not treated. Using a little hook, or sometimes their fingers, doctors lifted a person's eyelids. Most immigrants feared this exam. They knew that if trachoma were discovered, they would be sent back to their homeland. They also dreaded the exam because it was

A US Public Health doctor examines children upon arrival at Ellis Island.

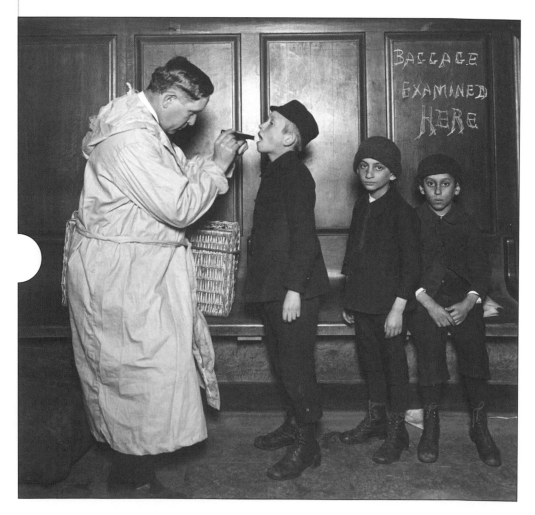

painful. One woman, who was five at the time, recalls being terrified. A man had jokingly told her that when they examined his eyes, one eyeball fell into his pocket.

When doctors suspected a problem, they marked the person's shoulder or back with chalk. Each medical condition was coded with letters. *CT* stood for trachoma, *Sc* for scalp infection, *H* for heart problems, and *X* for a suspected mental illness.

One woman remembers the fright of seeing a chalk mark on her sister's coat. "If they **deported** my sister," she thought, "where would she go?" Luckily, the little girl had a fancy coat with a silk lining. At the advice of a kind stranger, she turned her coat inside out. This saved her from being taken from the line for a closer inspection.

At Ellis Island, doctors had to determine if an immigrant was mentally as well as physically fit. To measure mental health and intelligence, they asked simple questions, such as

BITING BUGS

Lice were a common medical problem at Ellis Island. These biting bugs easily spread from person to person in the tightly packed ships and crowded immigration station. Lice not only made people itchy, they also spread a disease called **typhus**. With immigrants continuously coming in, it was difficult to rid the station of these blood-sucking insects.

"How much is two plus two?" One girl was asked if it were better to wash stairs from top to bottom or from bottom to top. The young girl did not understand that this was an intelligence question. She replied, "I don't go to America to wash stairs."

If doctors suspected mental illness or low intelligence, the people in question were asked to take special exams. Sometimes they had to put puzzles together. They also took memory tests. If immigrants failed the mental exams three times, they were rejected. Some inspectors felt that these exams were not always fair. There were immigrants who knew the answers but did not respond because they were frightened.

THE LEGAL INSPECTION

A legal inspection was another hurdle for immigrants. While awaiting their inspection, people crowded into the tremendous, flag-draped Registry Room. Each person was

This is a 1924 photo of the Registry Room at Ellis Island. The commotion and crowds in this "great hall" could make it a frightening place.

led to one of the bench-lined rows. Then they waited in the noisy hall for their names to be called.

At the head of each row an inspector sat behind a large desk on a high stool. Each inspector had a list from the

* * * *

steamship companies with information about passengers. Inspectors asked immigrants for their name, place of birth, age, occupation (job), and destination. Most people were headed for places where friends or family lived.

Inspectors also asked questions that needed a yes or no answer. A yes answer to certain questions could lead to deportation. One question was, "Have you ever been in jail?"

They also asked people if they already had a job waiting for them in America. Beginning in 1885, it was illegal for American employers to bring over workers. American

New arrivals line up to have their papers examined by inspectors.

workers did not want to lose their jobs to immigrants, who were willing to work for lower wages than Americans. Even low wages in America were higher than the wages most immigrants were earning in their homelands.

Some inspectors asked to see how much money an immigrant had. They wanted proof that immigrants had enough money to take care of themselves in America. To be safe, some people exchanged their second-class ticket

THIEVES

Bewildered immigrants on Ellis Island were easy prey for thieves. Crooks would come over from New York City disguised in official-looking caps and jackets. "May I help you with your suitcase?" they would ask a woman, who would never see her belongings again. "Let me see your money!" another would demand, taking an immigrant's fifty-dollar bill. "It's no good," the thief would say, giving him or her four bright pennies in return.

for third-class before leaving. This way they had extra money to show the inspector. For those who did not have the money, bills were sometimes passed from one person to another. "This had to be done with a quick motion of the hand so no one would get caught," a man remembered. Immigrants often helped each other in these trying moments.

THE BOARDS OF SPECIAL INQUIRY

Immigrants who did not pass the legal or medical inspections had to appear before a group of inspectors. These inspectors, who formed a board of special inquiry, made the final decision. Each board's three inspectors and an

Two immigrants face a board of special inquiry.

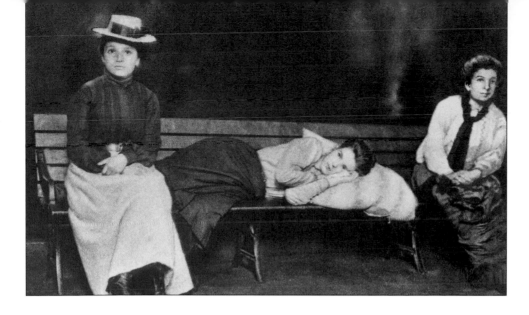

Sometimes immigrants were rejected by officials at Ellis Island. These three women are waiting for a steamship to take them back to their home country.

interpreter heard the cases of between fifty to one hundred immigrants each day.

One elderly woman, for example, could not figure out the puzzles. During the questioning, the woman convinced the board that she was worthy of admittance. She promised to show the inspectors that she could make them a delicious soup and could bake finer bread than they served on Ellis Island.

Not all cases turned out as well. One woman still remembers when the inspectors discovered that her grandmother had a black nail. "She raised us, all the years, with that hand and with that nail. There was nothing wrong with it. And they held her back . . . So we never saw her again . . . I'm still crying over it."

Only about 2 percent of the twelve million people who passed through Ellis Island were deported. But that amounted to about one quarter of a million people. Fiorello La Guardia, who later became mayor of New York City, was once an interpreter at Ellis Island. He wrote: "The immigration laws were rigidly enforced, and there

31

Some immigrants were held at Ellis Island for months. Here, a group of young detainees attend classes led by a social worker on the island.

AID FOR IMMIGRANTS

Groups called immigrant aid societies helped to ease the fear that gripped many immigrants. Members of aid societies explained problems when interpreters were unavailable. They assisted people in getting jobs and helped contact friends and relatives. They also did small favors, such as giving crackers, doughnuts, and milk to hungry children.

were many heartbreaking scenes on Ellis Island. I never managed . . . to become **callous** to the mental anguish, the disappointment, and the despair I witnessed almost daily."

WAITING ON THE ISLAND

The inspection process was often a whirlwind of fear and confusion. For many immigrants it only lasted a short while. Some immigrants, though, were **detained** on the island for days, weeks, or even months.

* * * *

People were detained for several reasons. About half of those detained were awaiting a hearing before a board of special inquiry. Others were recovering from illness in the hospital. Some were waiting for train fare to arrive from family or friends already in the country. Women and children under sixteen could not leave until a relative came for them.

Feeding all the detained people was a huge job. On busy days, the Ellis Island staff served three meals a day to three thousand people. During its six decades of operation, the food service quality varied. Some immigrants endured meals of rye bread and prunes served in dirty dining halls. Others were more fortunate. One woman still remembers a fish dinner with bread, butter, and big pitchers of milk. Foods such as white bread, gelatin, ice cream, hot dogs, and bananas were strange to many immigrants. Some people mistakenly ate bananas without peeling them first!

This photograph, taken in the early 1900s, shows immigrants having lunch at Ellis Island.

Sleeping conditions varied over the years as well. At times, bedbugs and lice tormented weary immigrants. People squeezed into narrow metal bunks stacked three rows high. In later, less crowded times, **detainees** slept comfortably on single beds with spotless blankets and sheets.

Immigrants gradually left Ellis Island. Relatives or needed funds arrived. People got well. Boards announced their decisions. Every morning inspectors read the names of those who were to be admitted to America. One man still remembers the moment when they called his family's name. Everyone jumped up and down and cried. That was all they wanted to hear.

This photograph shows the sleeping quarters as it looked in 1923. In busier years sleeping areas were not as comfortable.

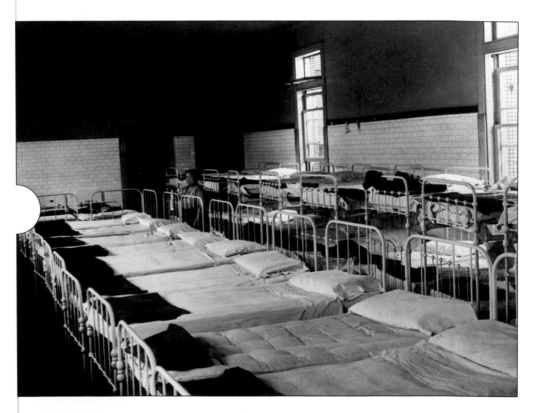

34

At times, Ellis Island had more people than it had space. This picture was taken in 1920, when the station was so crowded it had to be closed for a short time.

As the twentieth century rolled in, huge numbers of immigrants flocked to Ellis Island. Its busiest year was 1907, when about one million immigrants entered New York Harbor. On May 2, more than twenty-one thousand immigrants waited onboard ships. Dining halls, built to serve eight hundred, served three thousand at one meal. Inspectors said they felt swamped by a human tide, as they sometimes examined a stream of four to five hundred immigrants per day.

A WANING WELCOME

All Americans did not greet immigrants warmly in the 1900s. Some Americans were afraid of losing their jobs to immigrants, who would work for lower wages. Others disliked the "new" type of immigrant coming in. In the late 1800s most immigrants came from countries in northern and western Europe, including England, Ireland, Germany, Sweden, and Norway. During the twentieth century many

★ ★ ★ ★

A Hungarian mother and her children posed for this photo upon their arrival at Ellis Island in 1909.

came from southern and eastern European countries such as Italy, Russia, Poland, Hungary, and Austria.

In 1894, a group of wealthy Americans founded the Immigration Restriction League. These people felt that the "new" immigrants were "polluting" the blood of America. In response to the alarm and anger of groups like this one, Congress passed the Immigration Act of 1917. Thereafter, all immigrants aged sixteen and older would have to pass a

* * * *

reading test to be admitted into the United States. The league hoped that this test would block many immigrants from entry.

Four years later, Congress passed the Quota Law of 1921. This law set an overall **quota**, or limit, of about 358,000 immigrants per year. No more than 20 percent of a nation's yearly quota would be admitted in one month.

At the beginning of each month, ships raced to New York Harbor, hoping to get their passengers through. Sometimes the monthly quota was already filled. Then, people, who may have sold their homes and possessions for a ship's ticket, were turned back.

On July 1, 1922, the steamship *Conte Russo* sped into New York Harbor. After the First Quota Law of 1921, hopeful immigrants needed to arrive early to be included in the monthly quota.

By the mid-1920s, immigration was greatly reduced from that of the late 1800s. Here, immigrants are shown on the Lower East Side of New York City in 1890.

★ ★ ★ ★

Henry Curran, commissioner of Ellis Island in 1923, wrote about watching these immigrants depart. "Day by day the barges took them from Ellis Island back to the ships again, back to the ocean, back to what?" Some were carrying little American flags. Some were dressed up in their finest clothing "to celebrate their first glad day in free America." Most, he noticed, were softly weeping. "They twisted something in my heart that hurts to this day."

Even stricter laws were set by the Immigration Act of 1924. Total annual immigration was cut by about half to 164,677. The 1924 law also required immigrants to be examined, inspected, and approved in their native countries. American offices called **consulates** would supervise the process. This would prevent people from traveling thousands of miles only to be sent back. An Ellis Island official who recommended the change explained that it would save thousands of immigrants "the suffering we see at the Island daily, which is indescribable and that would melt a heart of granite."

By 1931, all of the overseas consulates were in place. Now, immigrants were brought to Ellis Island only in special

Here, the Registry Room, shown in 1954, has been cleared of furniture shortly before Ellis Island is shut down.

WAR SERVICE

During World War I few immigrants entered the United States because it was dangerous to travel overseas. Still, Ellis Island was not empty. The station held German and Austrian sailors captured in American harbors. Wounded American soldiers filled Ellis Island hospitals. Sailors also stayed on Ellis Island while waiting for their ships.

cases. There might be a child traveling alone, someone who got sick on the ship, or a foreign criminal who was caught trying to slip in.

In the year between June 1932 and June 1933, only about four thousand people were held at Ellis Island. Contrast this with one day—April 17, 1907—when the Ellis Island staff processed almost twelve thousand immigrants. An official inspecting Ellis Island in 1924 reported that the station looked like a "deserted village." Finally, in 1954 the once bustling station closed.

★ ★ ★ ★

Today, Ellis Island is preserved as part of the Statue of Liberty National Monument.

Visitors to the museum can use computers to research photos and ships' passenger records.

A NATION'S MONUMENT

Ellis Island's doorway did not stay closed forever. In 1965, President Lyndon Johnson made the former inspection station a national monument. As a national monument, Ellis Island would be preserved as a precious part of American history. It would also stand as a tribute to the strong-minded and brave-hearted people who made their way to America.

In 1990, the immigration station became the Ellis Island Immigration Museum. Exhibits, movies, and photographs record six decades of history. Visitors discover the stories of parents and grandparents who came in search of their future. The immigrants return too—but now they come in search of their past.

One eighty-year-old woman returned to Ellis Island in 1990. Again she became a ten-year-old child, climbing the wide steps into the towering station. She could see the worried faces. She could hear shouts and cries. She could feel the crowds and the confusion. Though seventy years had passed, it all came back to her.

ORAL HISTORY PROJECT

A fascinating section of the Immigration Museum is the Ellis Island Oral History Library. The Oral History Project began in 1973, when interviews with immigrants were tape-recorded and written down. More than twelve hundred people shared their experiences. Although many have since died, the Oral History Library preserves their memories. All of the words of the immigrants in this book were gathered from this American treasure.

The Immigration Museum tells the stories of the many immigrants who passed through its gates.

Glossary

callous—uncaring about others' suffering

consulate—a building where officials from another country work

contagious—easily spread from one person to another

deport—to send someone out of a country

detain—to delay or keep someone back

detainee—a person who is detained, or held back

entitled—able to secure a right according to law

explosives—materials that can burst or cause an explosion

immigrants—people who leave their native land to live permanently in another country

interpreter—a person who translates a language for someone who does not speak it

lice—wingless insects that live on animals and suck their blood

persecution—cruelty toward a person or group

quota—the highest number of people permitted admission from a group or nation

steerage—the bottom area of a ship containing steering equipment, where the lowest-paying passengers stay

stowaways—people who hide aboard a ship because they cannot pay for their passage

typhus—a disease spread by lice and fleas that causes severe headaches, high fever, and rashes

Timeline: Ellis Island

1890

Congress chooses Ellis Island as the site for New York's federal immigration station.

1891

The Immigration Act of 1891 creates the federal Bureau of Immigration, which sets up an inspection system.

1892

The immigration station opens on Ellis Island on January 1.

1897

A mysterious fire destroys the immigration station on June 14.

1900

The Ellis Island Immigration Station reopens on December 17.

1907

Almost 900,000 immigrants pass through Ellis Island.

1917

The Immigration Act of 1917 requires all immigrants sixteen years and older to be able to read in their native language.

1921 1924 1954 1965 1976 1983 1990

Quota Law of 1921 limits immigration to 357,803 per year, with no more than 155,000 from southern and eastern Europe.

The Immigration Act of 1924 limits immigration to 164,677 per year, allowing fewer than 25,000 from southern and eastern Europe.

The Ellis Island Immigration Station closes in November.

President Lyndon Johnson makes Ellis Island a part of the Statue of Liberty National Monument.

Ellis Island opens for National Park Service tours.

Restoration of Ellis Island begins.

The Ellis Island Immigration Museum opens on September 10.

To Find Out More

BOOKS AND FILMS

Bierman, Carol. *Journey to Ellis Island: How My Father Came to America*. New York: Hyperion Books for Children, 1998.

Freedman, Russell. *Immigrant Kids*. New York: Puffin Books, 1995.

Lawlor, Veronica. *I Was Dreaming to Come to America: Memories from the Ellis Island Oral History Project*. New York: Puffin Books, 1997.

Island of Hope—Island of Tears: The Ellis Island Immigration Museum Film. Guggenheim Productions, 1990.

ONLINE SITES

PBS Kids, Learning Adventures in Citizenship: Ellis Island
http://www.pbs.org/wnet/newyork/laic/episode4/topic2/e4_topic2.html

The Statue of Liberty—Ellis Island Foundation, Inc.
http://www.ellisisland.org/Immexp/index.asp?

Index

Bold numbers indicate illustrations.

Aid societies, 32

Barge Office, **13**, 13
Berlin, Irving, 9
boards of special
inquiry, **30**, 30–32
Bureau of Immigration,
11, 18–19

Castle Garden, 10, **11**
chalk markings, 25
consulates, 37

Deportation, 31, 38
detainees, 32–33
diseases, contagious,
19, 24

Ellis, Samuel, 13
Ellis Island, **4**, **12**, **40**
closing of, 39
conditions at, 21,
33–34
early history of, 13
entering, 18–23
fire at, 12–13
Immigration Museum,
40, 40–41, **41**
Oral History Library,
41

First-class passengers,
14, 20

Gilhooley, Michael, 18

Immigrants, **5**, **6**, **14**, **36**
belongings of, 4–5
rejection of, 11, 31
immigration, reasons
for, 6–7
Immigration Acts,
36–38
Immigration Restriction
League, 36–37
inspectors, 18–20, 23,
28, 30–32
interpreters, 31

Johnson, Lyndon, 40

La Guardia, Fiorello,
31–32
Lazarus, Emma, 22
legal inspections,
26–30, **28**
lice, 26, 34

Medical
examinations, **23**,
23–26, **24**
mental health, 25–26
money, 29–30
Mussolini, Benito, 7, **8**

New York, 10, 11

Oral History Project, 41

Quota Law, 37

Receiving stations,
10–13
Registry Room, 26,
26–**27**, **39**

Seaports, 10
second-class passengers,
14, 20
sleeping quarters, **34**
special inquiry, boards
of, **30**, 30–32
Statue of Liberty, **17**,
17–18, **22**
steamships, 15
steerage, 14–15
stowaways, 18

Theft, 30
tickets, types of, 14
travel conditions,
15–17, 21

World War I, 39

About the Author

Years of travel in natural and historic places have inspired and informed the work of author and photographer **Judith Jango-Cohen**. Visits to Ellis Island nurtured her interest in the remarkable story of immigration. Her thirty-four children's books reflect the depth of her experiences. They have been listed in Best Books for Children, recommended by the National Science Teacher's Association, and chosen for the Children's Literature Choice List.